Delacroix

CHARLES BAUDELAIRE

EUGENE DELACROIX
HIS LIFE AND WORK

Lear Publishers   New York

Delacroix, lake of blood by evil angels haunted,
Shadowed by a green wood's mad mysteries,
Where, under an angry sky in the night undaunted,
Pass stifled shadows, Weber's, to their destinies.

From *Les Phares* by Charles Baudelaire

To the Editor of *L'Opinion Nationale*.

Sir:

Once again I should like to pay homage—a supreme homage—to the genius of Eugene Delacroix. So I ask you to publish in your newspaper these few pages in which I shall try to cover, as briefly as possible, the evolution of his talent; the reason for his superiority, which in my opinion has not yet been sufficiently recognized; and finally, a few anecdotes and remarks concerning his life and character.

I had the good fortune to know the illustrious deceased when I was still very young (from 1845 on, if I remember correctly). In our relations, respect on my part and forbearance on his did not prevent mutual confidence and familiarity, and in the course of our friendship, I had ample time to obtain a most accurate idea not only of his method but also of the most intimate qualities of his great soul.

You must not expect me, sir, to give here a detailed analysis of the works of Delacroix. Apart from the fact that each one of us has done so to the best of his ability as the great painter revealed, one by one, the products of his creative brain, the list is so long that even if only a few lines were devoted to each of his principal works, such an analysis would almost fill a book. So I propose to give here an incisive resume of his work.

His monumental paintings are on display in the *Salon du Roi* at the Chamber of Deputies, in the library of the Chamber of Deputies, in the library of the Luxembourg Palace, in the Apollo Gallery of the Louvre, and in the Hall of Peace at the *Hotel de Ville*. These decorations embrace a vast number of allegorical, religious, and historic themes, all of them belonging to the noblest realm of the intelligence. As for his easel paintings, his drawings, grey monochromes, water-colors, etc., they reach an approximate total of 236 [later estimated at over 12,000. Ed.]

The big paintings shown at various annual exhibitions number 70. I derive this information from the catalogue which Theophile Silvestre has appended to his excellent essay on Eugene Delacroix in his volume entitled: *Story of Living Painters*.

I have myself tried more than once to draw up this enormous catalogue, but my patience has been exhausted by the painter's unbelievable fertility and I have been forced to give up the task. If Theophile Silvestre has erred, it has only been on the side of under-estimation.

I think, sir, that the important thing here is simply to seek out the characteristic quality of Delacroix's genius and to attempt to define it; to find out wherein he differs from his most renowned predecessors, while remaining their

equal; and to show finally, insofar as the written word makes it possible, the magic art thanks to which he was able to translate the *word* into plastic images more vivid and more appropriate than those of any other creator in the same profession—in short, to reveal the *special* faculty with which fate endowed Eugene Delacroix.

I

What is Delacroix? What was his role, his task in this world? That is the first question. I shall be brief. The Lowlands have Rubens; Italy has Raphael and Veronese; France has Lebrun, David, and Delacroix.

The superficial mind may, at first sight, be shocked by the association of these names, representing such different qualities and methods. But the more penetrating mind will see at once that all these painters have something in common, a kind of brotherhood or kinship deriving from their love of the great, the national, the vast, and the universal; a love that has always been expressed in so-called decorative painting or in large-scale *compositions*.

Many others, no doubt, have painted large-scale *compositions*, but those I have named did so in a way best fiitted to leave an eternal mark in man's memory. Who is the greatest of these men so great and so diverse? Each individual may

decide as he pleases, according to whether his temperament leads him to prefer the prolific, radiant, almost jovial abundance of Rubens; the sweet majesty and harmonious order of Raphael; the blissful and as-if-afternoon color of Veronese; the austere and taut severity of David; or the dramatic and almost literary eloquence of Lebrun.

None of the men can be replaced. All aiming at a similar goal, they used different means drawn from their personal endowment. Delacroix, the most recent in time, expressed with admirable vehemence and fervor what the others had not completely translated. Did some other quality perhaps suffer in the process, a quality which the others possessed? Possibly, but that is not the question at issue.

Many others beside myself have made a point of stressing the fatal consequences of an essentially personal genius; and after all, it is quite possible that the highest expressions of genius—not in the azure sky but on this poor earth where perfection itself is imperfect—have been achieved only at the expense of an inevitable sacrifice.

But no doubt, sir, you will ask: what is this mysterious *je ne sais quoi* which Delacroix, to the glory of our century, has translated better than any other artist? It is the invisible, the impalpable; it is the dream, the nerves, the *soul*. And he has done this—mark it well, sir—with no other means

12

save contour and color. He has done it better than anyone else; he has done it with the perfection of a consummate painter, with the discipline of a subtle writer, with the eloquence of a passionate musician. Moreover, it is one of the symptoms of the spiritual temper of our century that the arts strive, if not to supplement one another, at least to land each other new strength.

Delacroix is the most *suggestive* of all painters. His works, even his secondary and inferior paintings, give one the most to think about. They recall to the memory poetic emotions and ideas already known but which one thought forever buried in the night of the past.

Delacroix's work sometimes seems to me a kind of remembrance of the greatness and native passion of the universal man. This quite new and special merit of Delacroix, which enabled him with a simple contour to express man's gestures however violent, and with color create what might be called the atmosphere of the human drama. This striking originality has always won for him the sympathies of all poets, and if one could draw philosophical conclusions from a purely material phenomenon, I would ask you to observe, sir, that there were many more writers than painters in the throng gathered to pay their last respects to him. The blunt truth is that the painters have never completely understood him.

14

II

And after all, what is there really surprising in this? Do we not know that the time of the Michaelangelos, the Raphaels, the Leonardo da Vincis, even of the Joshua Reynoldses, has long since passed, and that the general intellectual level of artists has fallen markedly? It would no doubt be unfair to look among the artists of our time for philosophers, poets, and scholars; but it would be in order to ask them to show a little more interest than they do in religion, poetry, and science.

Outside of their studios what do they know? What do they like? What do they express? Eugene Delacroix was not only an artist in love with his craft. He was also a man of broad general culture, in contrast to other modern artists, most of whom are little more than famous or obscure daubers, sad specialists, and pure craftsmen, some able to paint academic figures, others fruit, and still others animals. Eugene Delacroix loved everything, could paint everything, appreciated all kinds of talents. His mind was open to all ideas and impressions: he enjoyed them in the most eclectic and the most impartial manner.

It goes without saying that he was an avid reader. His reading of poetry left in him grandiose and quickly defined images, ready-made pictures so to speak. However much he

16

differed from his master Guerin in method and color, he inherited from the great republican and imperial school a love of the poets and a kind of fierce spirit of competition with the written word. David Guerin, and Girodet were inspired by their reading of Homer, Virgil, Racine, and Ossian. Delacroix was the passionate translator of Shakespeare, Dante, Byron, and Ariosto. An important resemblance and a slight difference.

But let us penetrate a little more deeply into what might be called the master's teaching, a teaching which for me comes not only from the successive study of all his works and the simultaneous study of several of them at the Universal Exposition of 1855, but also from many conversations I had with him.

Delacroix was passionately in love with passion, and coldly determined to find ways of expressing passion in the most visible manner. In this dual approach we find, it may be said in passing, the mark of extreme genius which never calculates to please timorous souls who are easily satisfied and who find sufficient enjoyment in weak, soft, and imperfect works. An immense passion, combined with a formidable will—of such was Delacroix the man.

He used to repeat:

"Since I consider the impression transmitted by nature to

the artist the most important thing to be translated, must not the artist be armed in advance with all the most rapid means of translation?"

It is clear that in his eyes imagination was the most precious gift, the most important faculty which remained powerless and impotent if it did not have at its command a rapid skill which could follow its despotic and impatient whims. Certainly, he did not have to kindle the fire of his ever-incandescent imagination, but he always found the day too short to study means of expressing it.

To this ceaseless preoccupation one must attribute his constant researches with respect to color and the quality of colors, his curiosity about chemistry, and his conversations with manufacturers of colors. In that he was akin to Leonardo da Vinci who was also obsessed with the same curiosity.

Eugene Delacroix, despite his admiration for the passionate phenomena of life, will never be found in the company of that crowd of vulgar artists and writers who, in their limited intelligence, take refuge behind the vague and obscure word "realism." The first time I saw Delacroix—in 1845 I think (how the years pass, rapid and consuming!)— we talked of many commonplaces, that is, of the vastest yet simplest problems: of nature, for example. Here, sir, I take the liberty of quoting myself, for a paraphrase would not be

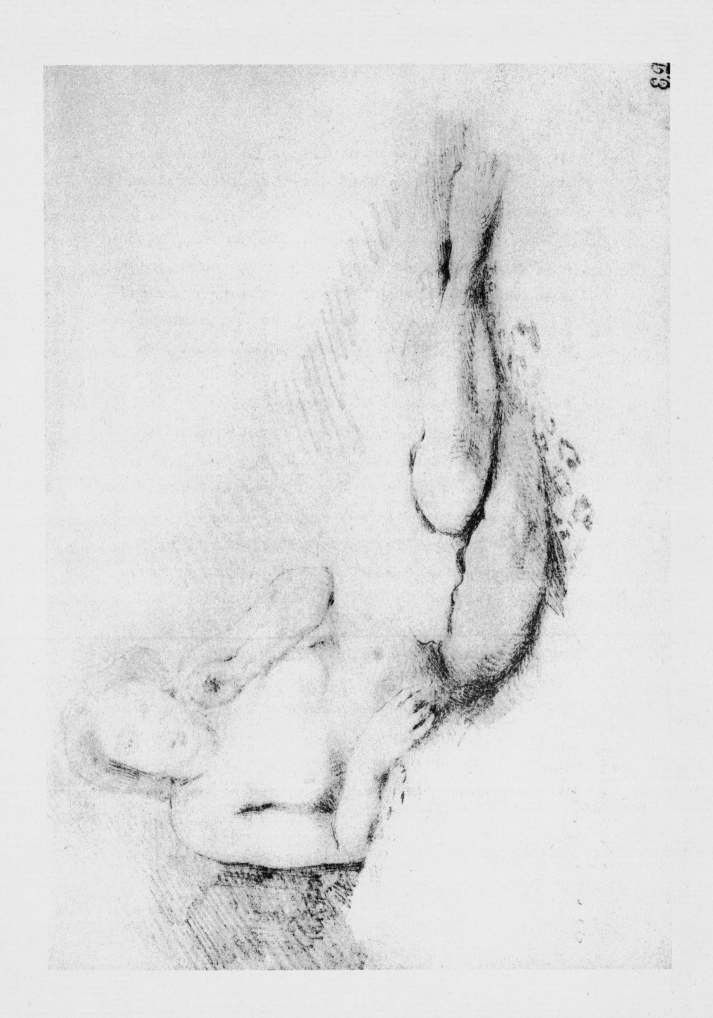

worth as much as the words I wrote years ago, almost at the master's dictation:

"Nature is only a dictionary, he often used to say. To understand the scope of the meaning implied in that sentence, one must recall the many ordinary uses of the dictionary. In it one looks for the meeting of words, their origin and etymology, and finally, one gets from it all the elements that go into a sentence or a story. But no one has ever considered the dictionary as a *composition*, in the poetic sense of the term. Painters who obey their imagination look in their dictionary for elements fitting in with their conception, and, adjusting them with a certain art, they give them an altogether new face. Those who have no imagination copy the dictionary. The result is a very great vice, the vice of banality, which is more particularly suited to those painters who specialize in what is called inanimate nature; for example, landscape painters, who usually consider it a triumph not to show their personality. By dint of observing and copying, they forget to feel and think.

"In this great painter, different people choose different aspects as the essence of his art. But all the component parts of his art were, or rather are, but the very humble servants of a unique and superior faculty. If very clean execution is necessary, it is in order that the dream may be very clearly

translated; if the execution is very quick, it is in order not to lose anything of the extraordinary impression accompanying the conception. The fact that the artist even pays attention to the material quality of his tools is also quite understandable, for all precautions have to be taken to make the execution swift and decisive."

Here let me say in passing that I have never seen a palette as minutely and as delicately prepared as that of Delacroix. It was like a skillfully arranged bouquet of flowers.

"In such a method, which is basically logical, all the human figures, their relative disposition, the landscape or interior which serves as their background or horizon, their clothing, in short, everything must serve to illuminate the general idea and bear its original color, its livery, so to speak. Just as a dream is placed in an atmosphere of color suited to it, so a conception, once it becomes a composition, must move about in an environment of color specifically its own. Obviously there is a special shade given to any one part of the picture: this becomes the key color and determines the others. Everyone knows that yellow, orange, and red inspire and represent ideas of joy, wealth, glory, and love; but there are thousand of yellow or red atmospheres, and all the other colors will be logically affected in a proportionate measure by the dominant atmosphere. The colorist's art is

24

obviously related in some respects to mathematics and music.

"Nevertheless his most delicate operations are the result of a feeling to which long practice has given unerring sureness. Clearly, this great law of general harmony rules out many examples of superficial brilliance and many crudities, even in the most famous painters. There are paintings by Rubens which make one think not only of colored fireworks, but of several sets of fireworks shot off from the same place. The larger a picture is, the broader the stroke must be. That goes without saying. But it is well that the strokes are not materially fused. They fuse naturally at a distance required by the sympathetic law that has associated them. Thus color obtains more energy and freshness.

"A good painting, faithful and equal to the dream that has engendered it, must be produced like a world. Just as the creation as we see it, is the result of several creations, with each one always completed by the one following it, so a picture, harmoniously constructed, consists of a series of superimposed pictures, each new layer giving more reality to the dream and causing it to rise a degree higher toward perfection. On the other hand, I recall having seen in the studios of Paul Delaroche and Horace Vernet vast paintings not sketched but begun—that is, completely finished in certain parts, while certain other parts still consisted of nothing

26

more than a black or white outline. This type of work might be compared with purely manual labor which must cover a specific quantity of space in a definite time, or a long road divided into a large number of sections. When one section is finished, it does not have to be re-done, and when the whole road is travelled the artist is delivered of his painting.

"All these precepts are of course more or less modified by the varying temperaments of individual artists. Nevertheless I am convinced that for rich imaginations it is the surest method. Consequently, too great deviations from this method attest to an abnormal and unfair importance attached to some secondary aspect of art.

"I do not fear that people will say it is absurd to conceive of one and the same method applied by a host of different individuals. For it is clear that rhetoric and prosody are not arbitrarily invented tyrannies but a collection of rules required by the very organization of the spiritual being; nor have prosody and rhetoric ever prevented the appearance of distinct originality. On the contrary, it would be far truer to say that they have aided originality to flower.

"For the sake of brevity I am forced to pass over a great many corollaries flowing from the main formula which contains, so to speak, all the formulas of true esthetics, and which may be expressed as follows: the whole visible universe is

only a storehouse of images and signs to which imagination assigns a relative place and value. It is a kind of food which imagination must digest and transform. All the faculties of the human spirit must be subordinated to the imagination which calls upon all of them at once. Just as knowing the dictionary well does not necessarily imply knowing the art of composition, and the art of composition itself does not imply universal imagination, so a *good* painter may be not a *great* painter; but a great painter must be a good painter, because universal imagination includes the knowledge of all means and the desire to acquire them.

"It is obvious that, in accordance with the ideas I have just tried to elucidate to the best my ability, the vast class of artists, that is, of men devoted to the expression of the beautiful, may be divided into two very distinct camps. The artist who calls himself a *realist* (since this word has a double meaning and has not been clearly defined, we prefer to call him a *positivist*, in order better to characterize his error) asserts: 'I wish to present things as they are, or as they would be even if I did not exist.' The other artist, the imaginative one, says: 'I wish to illuminate things with my spirit and project the refection to other spirits.' Although these two diameterically opposed methods may heighten or diminish all themes, from religious scenes to the most modest

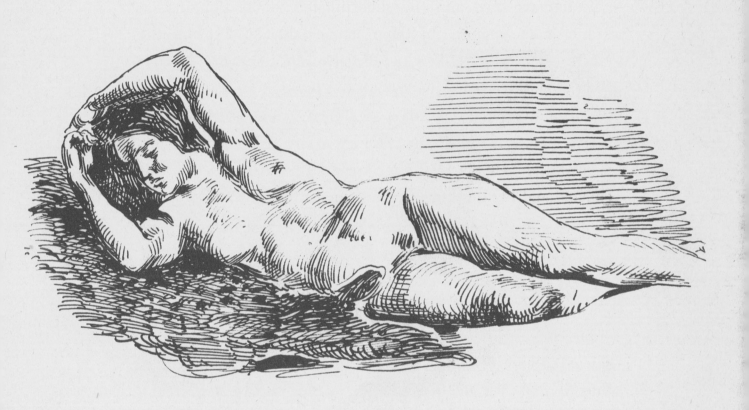

landscape, yet the man of imagination has generally been found in religious painting and in fantasy, while so-called *genre* painting and landscapes have seemed to offer vast resources to lazy minds that are not easily aroused. . . .

"Delacroix's imagination! It has never feared to scale the difficult heights of religion. Heaven belongs to it as does hell, as do war, Olympus, and sensuality. He is indeed the type of painter-poet! He is one of the chosen few, and the breadth of his mind includes religion in its domain. His imagination, glowing as a chapel ablaze with light, burns with every flame and every purple passion. All the sorrow there is in passion moves him. All the splendor there is in the Church illumines him. On his inspired canvases he pours in turn blood, light, and shadows. I think that he would like to add his natural splendor to the majesty of the Bible.

"I have seen a small *Annunciation* by Delacroix in which the angel visiting Mary was not alone but ceremoniously accompanied by two other angels. The effect of this heavenly court was charming and powerful. One of his youthful paintings, *Christ in the Garden of Olives* ('Lord, let this cup pass from me') shimmers with feminine tenderness and poetic unction. Sorrow and pomp, so heightened in religion, always find an echo in his spirit."

And more recently I wrote, concerning his last great work

32

in the Chapel of Holy Angels at Saint-Sulpice Church (*Heliodorus Driven from the Temple* and *Jacob Wrestling with the Angel*, a project that was so stupidly criticized):

"Never, not even in *Trajan's Mercy*, not even in the *Entry of the Crusaders into Constantinople*, has Delacroix revealed a more splendid and more skillfull supernatural coloring; never has he shown a more *consciously* epic design. I realize that some people, masons no doubt, or perhaps architects, have uttered the word *decadence* in connection with this last work. Here it is in order to point out that the great masters, poets or painters, Hugo or Delacroix, are always several years ahead of their timid admirers.

"The public, with respect to genius, is like a clock that is slow. Who among the clear-sighted does not realize that the master's first painting contained all the others in embryo? But that he unremittingly perfects his natural gifts, that he sharpens them with care, that he draws from them new effects, that he drives his own nature to the limit—that is inevitable, fatal, and praiseworthy. And it is precisely the chief hall-mark of Delacroix's genius that it does not know decadence. It only shows progress. But his initial qualities were so impetuous and so rich, they were so powerfully striking even to the most vulgar minds, that the latter are insensible to his daily progress. Only the serious-minded clearly perceive this.

34

"I spoke just a while ago of the remarks of a few *masons*. In using that term I meant the category of coarse and materialistic minds (their number is legion) who appreciate objects only in contour or, worse still, in their three dimensions: breadth, length, and depth, just as do savages and peasants. I have often heard persons of that ilk set up a hierarchy of qualities which to me is absolutely unintelligible. They assert, for example, that the faculty which enables one artist to create an exact contour or another a contour of supernatural beauty, is superior to the faculty which assembles contours in an enchanting manner. According to such people, color does not dream, it does not think, it does not speak. It would appear that when I look at the works of one of those men called colorists, I indulge in a pleasure which is not sublime in character. They are ready to call me a materialist, reserving for themselves the aristocratic epithet of spirtualists.

"These superficial minds do not realize that the two faculties can never be completely separated and that both are the result of an original germ that has been carefully cultivated. External nature only gives the artist an ever-recurring opportunity to cultivate this germ. It is but an incoherent mass of materials which the artist is asked to bring together and put in order, an *incitamentum*, an awakener of flaggering faculties. Speaking accurately, there is in nature

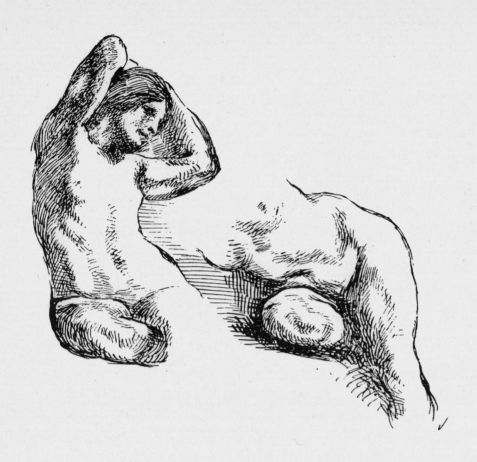

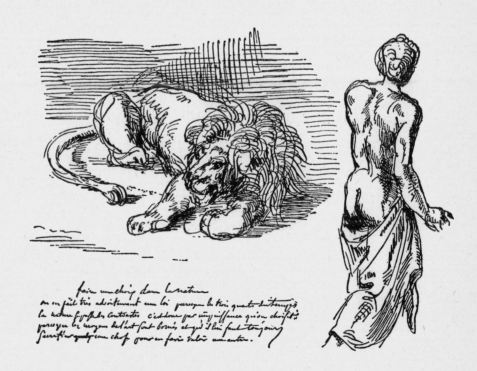

faire une chose dans la nature
on en fait très adroitement une loi parceque le trois quarts du temps
la nature y oppose des contrastes c'est donc par une puissance qu'on choisit
parceque les moyens de l'art sont bornés et qu'il lui faut toujours
sacrifier quelque chose pour en faire valoir un autre.

neither line nor color. These are two abstractions deriving their equal nobility from the same origin.

"Imagine a born artist as a child. He observes certain sinuosities in nature moving or at rest. From it he derives a certain voluptuousness and he enjoys capturing these impressions by drawing lines on paper, fondly exaggerating or lessening the curves. Thus he learns how to create emphasis, elegance, and character in a drawing. Imagine a child destined to perfect that aspect of art called color. It is from the clash or pleasing harmony of two colors and from the pleasure he thereby derives that he will acquire knowledge of the infinite combinations of color-tones. In both cases, nature has been pure stimulation.

"Line and color both make one think and dream. The pleasures deriving from them are of a different kind, but completely equal and absolutely independent of the theme of the painting.

"A picture by Delacroix, hung at too great a distance for you to judge the harmony of its contours and the more or less dramatic quality of its theme, already fills you with a kind of supernatural voluptuousness. You fell as if a magic atmosphere has walked toward you and enveloped you. Somber yet delightful, luminous yet tranquil, this impression, which remains indelibly engraved in your memory, proves

38

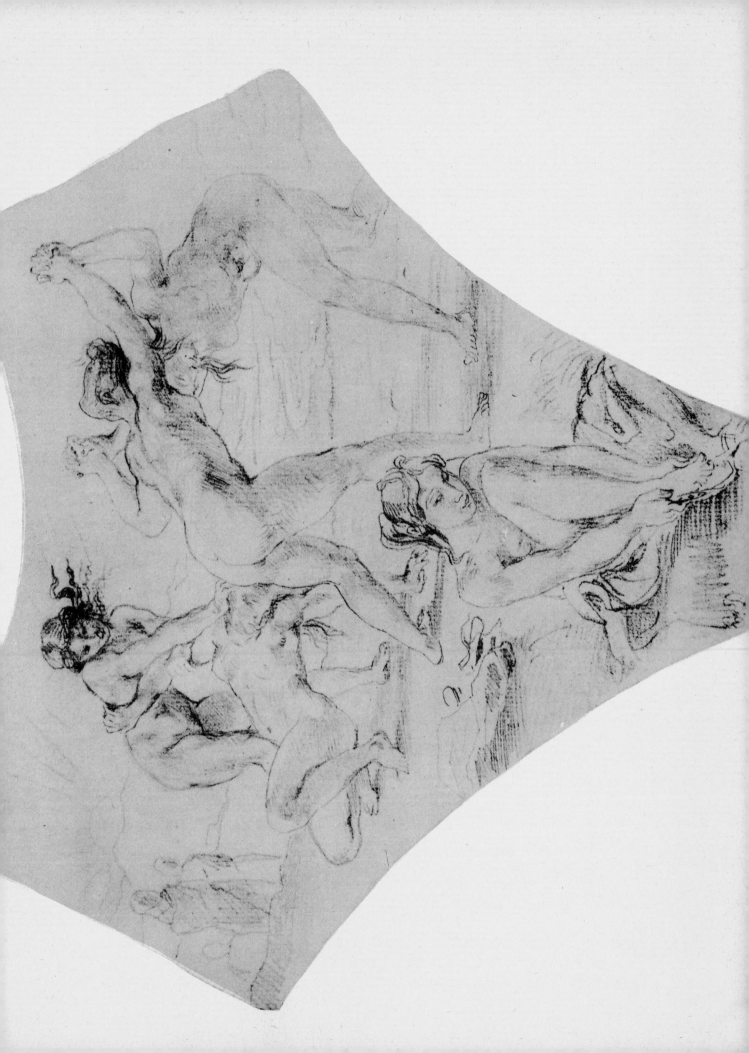

the true, the perfect colorist. And an analysis of the theme, when you draw closer, will neither add nor subtract anything from this initial pleasure, the source of which is elsewhere and far removed from any secret thought.

"I can give an inverse example. A well-drawn figure fills you with a pleasure that is quite alien to the theme. Voluptuous or terrible, this figure owes its charm solely to the arabesque it describes in space. The limbs of a tortured martyr, the body of a swooning nymph, if they are skillfully drawn, connote a type of pleasure in which the theme plays no part, and if you believe otherwise, I shall be forced to think that you are an executioner or a rake.

"But alas! What is the use of eternally repeating these useless truths?"

But perhaps, sir, your readers will appreciate, much more than this rhetoric, the details I am myself eager to give concerning the character and habits of our great departed painter.

IV

This dual nature of which I have spoken appears above all in the writings of Eugene Delacroix. As you know, many persons were amazed at the wisdom of his written opinions and the temperateness of his style, some regretting, other approving. His *Variations on the Beautiful*, his studies of Pous-

40

sin, Prud'hon, and Charlet, and other pieces published either in *L'Artiste*, then owned by M. Ricourt, or in the *Revue des Deux Mondes*, only confirm this dual character of great artists which drives them as critics to praise and analyze more lovingly the qualities they themselves need most as creators, and which serve as a foil to those they possess in super-abundance. If Eugene Delacroix had praised and glorified what we most admire in him, violence, suddenness of gesture, turbulent composition, and magic of color, then in truth we would have had reason to be amazed. Why look for what one has almost in excess? And how can one fail to praise what seems rarest and most difficult to acquire? We will always see the same phenomenon manifested in creators of genius, every time they apply their faculties to criticism. At the time of the great struggle between the two schools, the classical and the romantic, the simple-minded were dumbfounded to hear Eugene Delacroix ceaselessly laud Racine, La Fontaine, and Boileau. I know a poet of an ever violent and quivering temperament who is transported into a long ecstasy by a symmetrical and musically square line of Malherbe.

Moreover, however wise, meaningful, and clear-intentioned the literary fragments of the great painter appear to us, it would be absurd to think that they were written easily and with the sureness in execution of his brush. Just as he was

sure of *writing* what he thought on a canvas, so he was disturbed by his inability to *paint* his thoughts on paper. "The pen," he often said, "is not my tool. I feel that I think correctly, but the need of order which I am forced to obey, frightens me. Would you believe that the necessity of writing a page gives me a headache?" It is this embarrassment, caused by a lack of practice in writing, which may explain certain expressions—phrases that are a little hackneyed, a little *banal*, and even in the *Empire* manner—that too often escape his naturally distinguished pen.

What stamps Delacroix's style most visibly is conciseness and a kind of intensity without showiness, the habitual result of concentrating all his spiritual force on a given point. "The hero is he who is immovably centered," writes Emerson the moralist from across the sea, who, although he is supposed to be the head of the boring Boston school, has a certain Seneca-like quality which acts as a spur to meditation. "The hero is he who is immovably centered." This maxim, which the leader of the American Transcendentalists applies to one's conduct in life and business, may be similarly applied to the realm of poetry and art. One may also say: "The literary hero, that is, the true writer, is he who is immovably centered." One should therefore not be surprised that Delacroix had a very marked sympathy for concise and concentrated writers, those whose unadorned prose seems to imitate

the quick movements of thought and whose sentences resemble gestures. Montesquieu, for example. I can give you a curious example of this fertile and poetic brevity. Like myself, you have no doubt recently read in *La Presse* a very fine essay by Paul de Saint-Victor on the ceiling of the Apollo Gallery. Nothing is overlooked: the various conceptions of the Flood, the manner in which the legends bearing on the Flood should be interpreted, and the moral sense of the episodes and actions constituting the whole of this marvellous painting. And the painting itself is minutely described in that charming style, as witty as it is colorful, so many examples of which the author has given us. Yet the whole description will leave only a feeble trace in the memory, something like the very vague light of an enlargement. Compare this long piece with the few lines following, which I consider much more vigorous and much more apt *to give the sense of the painting*, even supposing that the painting they sum up does not exist. I am simply copying the program distrubted by M. Delacroix to his friends when he invited them to see the work in question:

APOLLO VICTOR OVER THE SERPENT PYTHON

"The god, mounted on his chariot, has already hurled some of his arrows. His sister, Diana, flying after him, hands him his quiver. Already pierced by the arrows of the god

of warmth and life, the bleeding monster writhes as it gives forth in fiery steam the last breath of its life and impotent rage. The waters of the flood begin to dry up, depositing dead bodies of human beings and animals on mountain peaks or dragging them in their wake. The gods are aroused at the sight of the earth abandoned to misshapen monsters, impure creatures of the slime. They have armed themselves like Apollo. Minerva and Mercury rush forth to exterminate the monsters until Eternal Wisdom re-peoples the solitary universe, Hercules crushes them with his club, Vulcan, god of fire, drives before him night and the impure vapors, while Boreas and the Zephyrs dry the waters with their breath and finally scatter the clouds. The nymphs of the rivers and streams have again found their bed of reeds and their urn which is still dirty from the mire and debris. More timid gods stand to one side watching this struggle of the gods and the elements. Nevertheless, Victory descends from the height of Heaven to crown Apollo the victor, and Iris, messenger of the gods, unfurls her scarf in the sky, symbol of the triumph of light over darkness and over the revolt of the waters."

I know that the reader will be forced to guess a good deal. He will have to collaborate, so to speak, with the writer of this passage. But do you really think, sir, that in this case admiration for the painter makes me imagine things? Am I completely wrong in asserting that here I see traces of aristo-

cratic habits formed by good reading, and of that straight-
forwardness of thinking which has enabled men of the world,
soldiers, adventurers, or even simple courtiers to write—
sometimes for there own amusement!—very fine books which
we professional writers are compelled to admire?

V

Eugene Delacroix was a curious mixture of skepticism,
politeness, dandyism, violent will, cunning, despotism, and
finally a kind of special kindness and quiet tenderness that
always goes hand in hand with genius. His father belonged
to that breed of strong men, the last of whom we knew in our
childhood—some, fervent followers of Jean-Jacques Rousseau, others, resolute disciples of Voltaire. All of them par-
ticipated with equal obstinacy in the French Revolution, and
the survivors, Jacobins or Cordeliers, rallied in perfect good
faith (an important point to be noted) to the standard of
Bonaparte.

Eugene Delacroix always retained traces of his revolution-
ary origins. Of him, as of Stendhal, it may be said that he
had a great fear of being duped. Skeptical and aristocratic,
he knew passion and the supernatural only by forcing himself to frequent the world of dreams. Hating crowds, he
looked upon them as little more than statue-breakers, and the

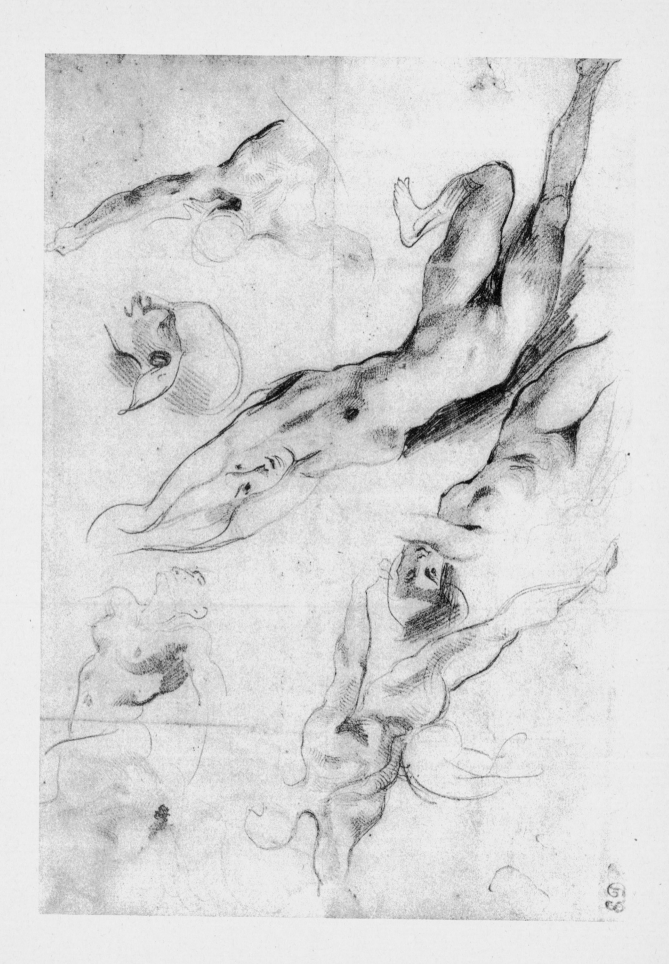

wanton damage done to a few of his works in 1848 was not calculated to convert him to the political sentimentalism of our time. There was even something in him—in his style, manners, and opinions—of Victor Jacquemont. I know that the comparison is somewhat insulting, hence I ask that it be interpreted only with the utmost moderation. There is in Jacquemont something of the enlightened bourgeois mind in revolt and a jesting spirit as fond of mystifying the priests of Brahma as those of Jesus Christ. Delacroix, guided by the taste that is always innate in a genius, could never indulge in such vulgarity. So my comparison refers only to the spirit of prudence and sobriety with which the two men were imbued. Similarly, the traits he inherited from the 18th century seemed borrowed above all from the class that was as far removed from the Utopians as it was from the wild-eyed—the class of polite skeptics, the victors and survivors, who in general owed more to Voltaire than to Jean-Jacques Rousseau. Thus, at first sight, Eugene Delacroix appeared to be simply an *enlightened* man, in the honorable sense of the term, a perfect *gentleman* without prejudices and passions. It was only after one came to know him well that one could penetrate the outer layer and divine the secret recesses of his soul. As for his outward bearing and manners, it would be more correct to compare him with M. Prosper Merimee. He had the same apparent and slightly affected coldness, the

same icy cloak covering over a shy sensitivity and an ardent passion for the good and the beautiful. Beneath the same seeming egotism there was the same devotion to secret friends and favorite ideas.

There was much of the *savage* in Eugene Delacroix. That was the most precious part of his soul, the part devoted entirely to painting his dreams and to the cult of his art. There was in him much of the man of the world. This aspect was designed to conceal the other and to obtain forgiveness for it. That, I believe, was one of the great preoccupations of his life, to hide the anger in his heart and not to look like a man of genius. His spirit of domination, a quite valid and even inevitable spirit, disappeared almost completely beneath his many kindnesses. He was like the crater of a volcano artistically hidden by bouquets of flowers.

Another mark of resemblance with Stendhal was his penchant for simple formulas, brief maxims, as guides to a good life. Like those all the more enamored of method in that their ardent and sensitive temperament seems to keep them further removed from it, Delacroix liked to draw up these little rules of practical morality which muddleheads and parasites, who practice nothing, contemptuously attribute to M. de la Palisse. But genius does not despise them because it is related to simplicity. They are strong, healthy, simple, and severe maxims, serving as shield and armor to one

plunged by the fatality of his genius into a never-ending battle.

Need I tell you that the some spirit of firm and disdainful wisdom inspired M. Delacroix's opinions on political matters? He believed that nothing was changing although everything seemed to be changing, and that certain decisive epochs in the history of peoples invariably produced analogous phenomena. His thinking in these matters, especially in its aspects of cold and bleak resignation, was very much akin to that of a historian for whom I have a very special fondness. You yourself, sir, so much at home in these questions, so capable of esteeming a man's talent even when he opposes you, you too, I am sure, have more than once been forced to admire him. I refer to M. Ferrari, the subtle and learned author of the *History of the Reason for the State.*

So the conversationalist who, in front of M. Delacroix, gave vent to childish utopian enthusiasms, soon felt the effect of his bitter laugh tinged with pitying sarcasm. And if one discussed in his presence the great chimera of modern times, the over-inflated notion of continuous perfectibility and perpetual progress, he would sharply ask: "Then where are your Phidiases? Where are your Raphaels?"

But do not think that this blunt common sense stripped M. Delacroix of any grace. His lively skepticism and his refusal to be duped seasoned like a Byronic salt, his highly poetic

and colorful conversation. From himself—that is, from his own genius and the consciousness of his genius—rather than from his long experience as a man of the world, he acquired a marvellous sureness and ease of manner. His politeness, like a prism, tolerated all nuances, from the most cordial affability to the most irreproachable impertinence. He had at least twenty different ways of saying: "My dear sir!", and to a trained ear they ran the gamut of sentiment. Here I must add, for I consider it a new motive for praise, that Eugene Delacroix, although—or rather—because he was a complete man of genius, had much of the dandy about him. He himself confessed that in his youth he had indulged with pleasure in the most materialistic vanities of dandyism, and he told with a laugh but not without a certain pride that, together with his friend Bonnington, he had labored diligently to inculcate in the elegant young people a taste for the English cut in shoes and clothes. This detail will not, I hope, be considered insignificant, for when one has to depict the nature of certain men no memories are superfluous.

I have already said that the attentive observer was struck above all by the natural part of Delacroix's soul, despite the deadening veil of a refined civilization that covered it. Everything in him was energy, but energy flowing from the nerves and the will, for physically he was frail and delicate. The tiger poised for its prey has less fire in its eyes and less im-

patient quiverings in its muscles than our great painter showed when his whole soul had hit upon an idea or sought to capture a dream. Even the physical characteristics of his face, his Peruvian or Malayan skin, his large black eyes narrowed by intense concentration and as if drinking in the light, his thick and shiny hair, his stubborn forehead, his tightly shut lips conveying an expression of cruelty as a result of the constant straining of his will—in fact, his whole being suggested that he was of exotic birth. More than once, as I looked at him, I thought of the ancient kings of Mexico, of Montezuma whose practiced hand could in a single day sacrifce three thousand human creatures on the pyramid-like Altar of the Sun; or of one of those Hindu princes who, amid the splendors of the most lavish festivals, reveals a kind of unsatisfied avidity and an inexplicable nostalgia in the depths of his eyes, something akin to remembrance and regret of things not known. I ask you to observe how the general color in Delacroix's paintings is similar to the color in Oriental landscapes and interiors, and how it produces a sensation analogous to that felt in semi-tropical countries where a tremendous diffusion of light gives an almost crepuscular impression to the sensitive eye, despite the intensity of the local color-tones. The moral in his works, if one may be permitted to speak of morality in painting, also bears a visibly Moloch-like stamp. Everything in his work is only desolation,

62

massacres, conflagrations. Everything bears witness to man's eternal and incorrigible barbarism. Cities smoking and in flames, slaughtered victims, raped women, even children hurled under horses' hooves or cringing under the dagger of delirious mothers—all his work, I say, resembles a terrible hymn composed in honor of doom and irremediable sorrow. Certainly, he was not lacking in tenderness, and at times he wielded his brush to express tender and voluptuous sentiments. But here, too, incurable bitterness was spread in heavy doses, and nonchalance and joy (the usual companions of naive voluptuousness) were absent. Only once, I believe, did he attempt the droll and the comic, and, as if sensing that that was beyond and below his nature, he never tried again.

VI

I know several people who have the right to say: *"Odi profanum vulgus"* ("I hate the rabble"). But which of them can add triumphantly: "Et arceo" ("And keep it at a distance")? Too many handshakes debases one's character. If ever a man had an *ivory tower* well guarded by bars and locks, it was Eugene Delacroix. Who has more deeply loved his *ivory tower*, that is, privacy? I think that he would have gladly armed it with cannon and removed it to a forest or an inaccessible peak. Who has more deeply loved his *home*, sanctuary and lair? As others seek privacy for their de-

bauches, he sought privacy for inspiration and literally re-
velled in work. "The one prudence in life is concentration;
the one evil is dissipation," writes the American philosopher
we have already quoted.

Delacroix could have written that maxim, and indeed, he
practiced it austerely, He was too much a *man of the world*
not to despise the world, and the efforts he spent not to be
too visibly *himself* led him naturally to prefer our company.
Our does not only mean the humble writer of these lines.
It also means several others, old or young, journalists, poets,
and musicians, with whom he could freely relax and give
vent to his true feelings.

In his delightful essay on Chopin, Liszt includes Delacroix among the most assiduous visitors of the poet-musician,
and says that the painter loved to dream to the sounds of that
light and passionate music which is like brilliant bird dancing
over an abyss.

Thus thanks to the sincerity of our admiration we were
able, although still very young, to penetrate that so closely
guarded studio. Inside, despite our severe French weather,
an equatorial climate prevailed. The eye was immediately
struck by the sober solemnity and the austerity so typical
of the old school. In our early childhood we remember having
seen studios of some of the old rivals of David, touching
heroes who have long since passed away. One felt that this

31 janvier 60.

retreat could not be inhabited by a frivolous mind, titillated by a thousand senseless caprices.

In it there were no rusty coats of mail, no Malay daggers, no old Gothic ironwork, no jewels, no knick-knacks, no bric-a-brac, nothing that reveals the owner as one who likes toys and the imaginery roaming world of childhood dreams. A marvellous portrait by Jordaens he had dug up somewhere or other, and a few sketches and copies made by the master himself were all that decorated his spacious studio illuminated by a soft and gentle light.

These copies will probably be on display at the sale of Delacroix drawings and paintings which, I am told, is to take place next January. He had two very diffeffrent manners in copying. One was free and broad, an equal mixture of faithfulness and betrayal, in which he put a good deal of himself. This method resulted in a charming bastard compound, imbuing the mind with pleasing uncertainty. This, paradoxically enough, was the impression I got from a large copy of Ruben's *Miracles of Saint Benedict*. In his other manner, Delacroix became the most obedient and humble slave of his model, and he achieved an exactness of reproduction which only those who have seen these miracles can believe. This group includes, for example, copies he made of two heads by Raphael in the Louvre, in which the expression, style, and manner are imitated with such perfect naivete

that is is difficult to ascertain which are the originals and which the reproductions.

After a midday meal lighter than that of an Arab, his palette meticulously prepared with the care of a flower-girl or an expert in window-display, Delacroix sought to continue his interrupted train of thought. But before plunging into his stormy labors, he often had moods of lassitude, fears, and fits of nerves, reminding one of the Pythoness fleeing the god, or of Jean-Jacques Rousseau fidgeting and fumbling with books and papers for an hour before putting pen to paper. But once the artist's imagination was kindled, he did not stop until he was overcome by sheer physical weariness.

One day, as we were discussing a question that always interests artists and writers, the proper hygiene for working and living, he said to me:

"Formerly, in my young days, I could not get down to work unless I could look forward to a pleasant evening—a concert, dance, or any other kind of amusement. But today I am no longer like a schoolboy. I can work without stopping and without any hope of reward. And then," he added, "if you knew how tolerant and easily satisfied with small pleasures diligent work makes a person. The man who has done a good day's work will find enjoyment enough in sitting down with the corner storekeeper and playing cards with him."

This remark made me think of Machiavelli playing at dice

with the peasants. One day, it was a Sunday, I noticed Delacroix at the Louvre accompanied by his old servant, a woman who has devotedly taken care of him for thirty years. He, the elegant and refined erudite, did not consider it below his dignity to explain the mysteries of Assyrian sculpture to that wonderful old lady who listened to him with unfeigned attentiveness. Once again I immediately thought of Machiavelli and of our former conversation.

The truth is that in the last years of his life, everything called pleasure had forsaken him. He knew but one rule, a single, harsh, exacting, and terrible rule—work. Work was now more than a passion. It might have been called a frenzy.

After devoting the hours of his day to painting, either in his studio or on the scaffolds, he mounted to paint his large decorative works, Delacroix still found strength enough to fall back on his love of art. He counted that day badly spent if his evening hours were not given over to drawing by the corner of the fire beneath a lighted lamp. He would cover the paper with dreams, sketches, figures haphazardly encountered in his life. Sometimes he would copy drawings by other artists whose temperament was the furthest removed from his own. For he had a passion for notes and sketches, and he indulged in this passion wherever he was. For quite a long time he had a habit of sketching at the home of friends where he spent his evenings. That is why M. Villot owns a

considerable number of excellent sketches from that fertile pen.

Once he said to a young man I know: "If you are not skillful enough to sketch a man jumping out of a window in the time it takes him to fall from the fourth story to the ground, you will never be able to produce great works." Here I find metaphorically expressed the obsession of his whole life, to execute quickly enough and with sufficient sureness so as not to allow any element in the intensity of an act or idea to be lost.

Delacroix was, as many others have observed, a conversationalist. But the amusing thing is that he was afraid of conversation as if it were a debauch, a dissipation in which he risked squandering his energies. When you came to see him, he began by saying:

"We won't talk this morning, will we? Or only very little, very little."

And then he chatted for three solid hours. His conversation was brilliant, subtle, but full of facts, memories, and anecdotes—in short, meaty conversation.

When he was aroused by opposition, he would draw back momentarily. Then, instead of assailing his adversary frontally, a tactic that risked substituting the rougher methods of the auditorium for the skirmishes of the drawing-room, he would play with his opponent for a while and then resume

74

his attack with unexpected arguments or facts. It was the conversation of a man who loved struggle, but a slave to courtesy, shrewd, deliberately yielding, replete with sudden retreats and attacks.

In the intimacy of his studio, he liked to relax and even give his opinion about painters who were his contemporaries. On such occasions we often had to admire the graciousness of his genius, springing perhaps from a special kind of naivete or faculty for enjoyment.

He had an astonishing weakness for Decamps, who is considered quite mediocre today but of whom his mind had no doubt retained powerful memories. The same was true of Charlet. He purposely sent for me once, in order to give me a vehement *dressing-down*, in connection with an irreverent article I had written about that spoiled child of chauvinism. In vain I sought to explain to him that I was not criticizing the Charlet of the first period but the Charlet of the decadence; not the noble historian of Napoleon's old soldiers but the clever cafe-wit. He never forgave me for that.

He admired certain aspects of Ingres, and indeed he needed a powerful critical sense to admire with his reason what his temperament led him to reject. He even carefully copied photographs made from some of those detailed pencil-portraits, where one best appreciates Ingres' solid and in-

cisive talent, all the more nimble for working in a more crowded space.

Horace Vernet's horrible color did not prevent him from feeling the personal virtuosity in most of his paintings. Delacroix found amazing expressions to praise Vernet's surface brilliance and tireless energy. His admiration for Meissonier went a little too far. He had taken possession, almost by violence, of the preparatory drawings made for *The Barricade*, Meissonier's finest painting. And as a matter of fact, Meissonier expressed his talent much more vigorously with a simple pencil than with a brush. Of Meissonier, Delacroix often said, as if dreaming uneasily of the future: "After all, of us all, he is the surest to live!" Is it not curious to see the creator of such great things almost jealous of the man who only excelled in little things?

The only man whose name could evoke harsh words from his aristocratic lips was Paul Delaroche. He found no excuse for the latter's works, and he had an indelible memory of the way he had suffered from Delaroche's dirty and bitter painting—*done with ink and shoe-polish*, as Theophile Gautier once said.

But the one with whom he liked best to engage in lengthy conversations was the man least like him in talent as well as ideas, in complete antithesis to himself. This man has not yet received his due; and his brain, although misty like the

smoke-filled sky of his native city, contains a host of admirable things. I mean Paul Chenavard.

The abstruse theories of the philosophical painter of Lyons
made Delacroix smile, and the abstract pedagogue considered
the delights of pure painting to be frivolous if not blame-
worthy. But as far apart from each other as they were, and
precisely because they were so far apart, they liked to draw
near to each other. They were like two boats fastened by
grappling-hooks, unable to pull apart. Both of them, moreover, very cultured and endowed with a remarkable sense
of sociability, met on the common ground of erudition.
This is not in general the field in which artists shine.

So Chenavard was a rare source of stimulation to Delacroix. It was really a pleasure to see them clash in an innocent
struggle, the words of the one lumbering heavily like an
elephant in full battle array, the words of the other gleaming
like a rapier and just as sharp and flexible. In the last hours
of his life, our great painter expressed the desire to shake
the hand of his friendly opponent. But the latter was then far
from Paris.

VII

Sentimental and sophisticated ladies will perhaps be
shocked to learn like Michelangelo (remember the closing
line of one of his sonnets; Sculpture! Divine Sculpture, you

80

are my only beloved!), Delacroix made Painting his only muse, his only mistress, his sole and self-sufficient voluptuous-ness.

No doubt he had loved many women in the turbulent hours of his youth. Who has not sacrificed too much to that formid-able idol? And who does not know that those who have served it best complain of it the most? But long before his death, he had expelled women from his life. Had he been a Moslem, he would not perhaps have driven them out of the mosque, but he would have been astonished to see them enter it, since he could not understand what kind of a conversation they could have with Allah.

In this question as in many others, Oriental ideas got the upper hand in him in vivid and despotic fashion. He con-sidered woman an *objet d'art,* delightful and suitable for exciting the mind, but a disobedient and disturbing *objet d'art.* If permitted to cross the threshold of one's heart, she would ravenously devour one's time and strength.

I remember once in a public place I showed him the face of a woman of original beauty and melancholy nature. He was quite willing to savor her beauty but as for the rest, he said to me with a quick laugh: "How do you expect a woman to be melancholy?", implying no doubt that woman lacks an essential *something* to know the sentiment of melancholy.

That is, unfortunately, a very uncomplimentary theory, and I should not like to preach insulting opinions about a sex that has so often demonstrated fervent virtues. But you will at least grant me that it is a prudent theory. Nor can talent be too heavily armed with prudence in a world of pitfalls and the man of genius is privileged to maintain certain doctrines (provided they do not disturb the order of things) which, in a mere citizen or family man, would scandalize us.

I may add, at the risk of casting a shadow on his memory, in the opinion of some sad souls, that he did not show any tender weaknesses toward children either. Childhood symbolized to his mind hands covered with jam (thus soiling linen and paper), loud beating on a drum (which disturbed one's concentration), or playing with fire and as slyly dangerous as a monkey.

"I distinctly remember," he sometimes said, "that when I was a child, *I was a monster*. Consciousness of duty is acquired very slowly, and it is only through sorrow, punishment, and the progressive use of his reason that man diminishes little by little his natural cruelty."

Thus, using plain common sense, he returned to the Catholic idea. For one may say that in general the child, relative to the man, is much closer to original sin.

No 1156 du Catalogue de la
Vente E. Delacroix
Compositions diverses

VIII.

It was as if Delacroix had reserved all his sensitivity, which was masculine and profound, for the austere sentiment of friendship. There are people who easily grow fond of a chance acquaintance. Others reserve this sublime faculty for great occasions. The famous man about whom I write with so much pleasure did not like to be disturbed for little things, but if important things were involved, he became helpful, courageous, and ardent. Those who knew him well could appreciate on many occasions his very English loyalty, correctness, and steadfastness in social relations. If he was demanding toward others, he was no less severe toward hisself.

I can only speak with sadness and ill temper of certain accusations levelled aginst Eugene Delacroix. I have heard people accuse him of selfishness and even avarice. Please note how this reproach is always made by the numerous class of banal spirits against those who strive to maintain their generosity on the same high level as their friedship.

Delacroix was very economical. That was the only way in which he could be, on occasions, very generous. I could prove this by several examples, but I hesitate to do so without having been authorized by him or by those who have had reason to be grateful toward him.

Note too that for many years his paintings sold very badly. His decorative works absorbed almost his entire income. Sometimes he had to pay for them out of his own pocket. Many times he proved his contempt for money when poor artists showed the desire to own one of his works. Then, like a generous and liberal-minded doctor who sometimes demands fees and sometimes donates his services gratis, he would give away his paintings or sell them at any price.

Finally, sir, note that the superior human being is forced to defend his own person more than anyone else. One may say that all society is at war with him. This rule has been more than once verified. His politeness is called coldness; his irony, however attenuated, is called cruelty; his economy, avarice. But if on the contrary the unfortunate being proves reckless, society, instead of pitying him, declares: "He has deserved it. His poverty is the punishment of his loose living."

I may state that in the matter of money and savings, Delacroix completely shared Stendhal's opinion, an opinion that combines loftiness with prudence.

"The man of talent," wrote the latter, "must see to it that he gets what he absolutely needs so as not to depend on anyone (in Stendhal's day, this was an annual income of 6,000 francs); but if, once he has obtained this guarantee, he wastes his time in increasing his fortune, he is a wretch."

Quest of the necessary and contempt of the superfluous—
that is the way of life of a wise man and a stoic.

One of the chief preoccupations of our painter in the last
years of his life was the judgment of posterity and uncertainty as to the fate of his works. Sometimes his sensitive
spirit would glow with the thought of immortal glory. Sometimes he spoke bitterly of the fragility of his canvases and
colors. On other occasions he cited with envy the old masters
almost all of whom had the good fortune to be reproduced
by clever engravers, capable of adapting the style of their
engravings to the nature of their originals, and he deeply
regretted not having found someone to reproduce his works.
The destructibility of a work of painting compared with the
solidity of a work of literature was an ever-recurring theme
in his conversation.

When this man, so frail and so obstinate, so nervous and
so brave, this unique figure in the history of European art,
this sickly and delicate artist who constantly dreamed of
covering walls with his grandiose conceptions, was struck
down by a chest inflammation of which he seems to have had
a fatal foreboding, we all felt the same kind of depression,
the same sensation of heightened lonliness we had already
experienced at the death of Chateaubriand and of Balzac.
Only recently we again had this sensation at the disappearance
of Alfred de Vigny. In a great national bereavement there is

a lowering of general vitality, a darkening of the intellect resembling a solar eclipse—a momentary imitation of the end of the world.

Yet I believe that this impression affects especially those solitary figures on the heights whose only family ties can be formed along their intellectual friendships. As for the other citizens, most of them find out only by degrees what the nation has lost in losing a great man, and what a vacuum he has created in leaving them. Even then, they have to be told what they have lost.

I thank you, sir, with all my heart for having been good enough to allow me to draw freely on my memories of one of the rare geniuses of our unhappy century—so poor and rich at the same time, sometimes too exacting, sometimes too indulgent, and too often unjust.

Paris 1863

(Translated from the French by Joseph M. Bernstein)

LEAR BOOKS